Bible Readers Series

A Study of Galatians

SET FREE BY GOD'S GRACE

William Carter

Abingdon Press / Nashville

SET FREE BY GOD'S GRACE
A STUDY OF GALATIANS

ISBN 0-687-02045-X

03 04 05 06 07 08 09 10 11 12—10 9 8 7 6 5 4 3 2 1
Manufactured in the United States of America.

CONTENTS

Chapter One

1

DELIVERED FROM BONDAGE

PURPOSE

To challenge us to live in the freedom that the gospel of Christ offers

BIBLE PASSAGE

Galatians 1:6-7

6 I am astonished that you are so quickly deserting the one who called you in the grace of Christ and are turning to a different gospel— 7 not that there is another gospel, but there are some who are confusing you and want to pervert the gospel of Christ.

Galatians 2:11-21

11 But when Cephas came to Antioch, I opposed him to his face, because he stood self-condemned; 12 for until certain people came from James, he used to eat with the Gentiles. But after they came, he drew back and kept himself separate for fear of the circumcision faction. 13 And the other Jews joined him in this hypocrisy, so that even Barnabas was led astray by their hypocrisy. 14 But when I saw that they were not acting consistently with the truth of the gospel, I said to Cephas before them all, "If you, though

5

a Jew, live like a Gentile, and not like a Jew, how can you compel the Gentiles to live like Jews?"

15 We ourselves are Jews by birth and not Gentile sinners; 16 yet we know that a person is justified not by the works of the law but through faith in Jesus Christ. And we have come to believe in Christ Jesus, so that we might be justified by faith in Christ, and not by doing the works of the law, because no one will be justified by the works of the law. 17 But if, in our effort to be justified in Christ, we ourselves have been found to be sinners, is Christ then a servant of sin? Certainly not! 18 But if I build up again the very things that I once tore down, then I demonstrate that I am a transgressor. 19 For through the law I died to the law, so that I might live to God. I have been crucified with Christ; 20 and it is no longer I who live, but it is Christ who lives in me. And the life I now live in the flesh I live by faith in the Son of God, who loved me and gave himself for me. 21 I do not nullify the grace of God; for if justification comes through the law, then Christ died for nothing.

CORE VERSES

I have been crucified with Christ; and it is no longer I who live, but it is Christ who lives in me. And the life I now live in the flesh I live by faith in the Son of God, who loved me and gave himself for me. (Galatians 2:19b-20)

OUR NEED

Each summer I teach in schools of Christian mission. One summer, the text for the spiritual life study was written by Phillip Peter and Barbel Wartenberg-Potter. It was entitled *Freedom Is for Freeing* and was on the Letter to the Galatians. This book brought me new understanding of the depth of the freedom we have in Christ. Here is an excerpt:

The story of the rich young man is an example of how Jesus and Paul understood law and gospel in relation to rich and poor (Mk. 10:17-31).

The young man comes to Jesus with the sincere question: "What must I do to inherit eternal life?" Jesus reminds him of the ten commandments, the law of Moses, as his guide. The young man says, "I have been doing it, all of it." In a literal way he has been keeping the law, but this did not fulfill his search for "life," real life, life of eternity, life with integrity, purpose and compassion. Paul would say: The law did not justify him (that is, put his relations with God and others in order). Now Jesus leads him to the test: Is he ready for the self-giving love and sharing of what he had and is, for a life of discipleship? But the young man is not ready. Many of us are not ready. He is not free to follow Jesus; his heart is bound to property, to himself and his belongings. Property in itself is not evil or bad. But it has the power to occupy our hearts, bind our minds to moneymaking, profits, savings and stock maneuverings.[1]

The young man could not find deliverance from bondage in his faithful adherence to religious and moral law. Yet he was unable to accept the deliverance Jesus offered. In this chapter, we will consider Paul's radical understanding of Christian deliverance. For various reasons, it is still difficult for many contemporary seekers to accept the freedom offered in Jesus Christ.

FAITHFUL LIVING

The letter to the church at Galatia is believed to be the first written statement of the extraordinary freedom bestowed in Christ. Therefore, Galatians ranks as one of the most important documents in the history of Christianity. It merits continual study.

The letter was probably written around A.D. 55, a couple

of years after Paul's first visit to Galatia. Our Bible Passage is drawn from the first two chapters. In this passage Paul describes his problem with the established leaders of the new movement and states his conviction concerning the primacy of faith.

Although this may be the first time the doctrine was written down, it was obviously not the first time that justification by faith had been preached. Paul began the letter by expressing his disappointment that some of the Galatian Christians had already forgotten the gospel of grace they had heard. They were turning to other gospels, versions preached by those who confused priorities. As we read on, we learn that Paul was arguing against leaders like Peter and James and against evangelists sent out by them.

Paul went directly to the heart of the matter. The Galatian Christians were not to believe any other version of the gospel even if it was preached by an angel or by one of those people from Jerusalem or by Paul himself. Anyone who preached anything other than salvation by grace should be accursed, the apostle claimed.

Now Paul had met with the Jerusalem group. Some three years after he encountered Christ, he visited with Peter and James, though he seems to have been unimpressed by the meeting (Galatians 1:18-19). Eleven years later he joined in a conference in Jerusalem where he defended his mission to the Gentiles and received approval (2:10). Paul made it clear, however, that his commission as an apostle came, not from Jerusalem, but from Jesus Christ.

To further his point, Paul went on to tell the story of how he confronted Peter at Antioch when Peter refused to eat with Gentile Christians while other Jews were present (Galatians 2:11-14). Paul said that even his friend Barnabas, appointed by the Jerusalem group as pastor at Antioch, refused to eat. Likewise, all the other Jews kept apart. And Paul? He denounced them all as hypocrites and legalists.

Why did Paul get so excited about such a small thing?

Paul got so excited because it was not small. The very essence of the gospel of Jesus Christ is that we are free of restraints on with whom we eat. If we do not accept one another, we cannot understand the Christian faith. If we cannot throw off the ancient dietary requirements, then how can we possibly put on the garments of the new creation? As Paul put it, "If I build up again the very things that I once tore down, then I demonstrate that I am a transgressor" (Galatians 2:18).

We cannot substitute one legalism for another. We can no more have "rules for becoming a Christian" than we can expect to get a blessing from the Lord because we have laid a new lamb on the altar. The only thing we have to give is ourselves (Remember Romans 12:1.).

Paul said, "We ourselves are Jews by birth and not Gentile sinners; yet we know that a person is justified not by the works of the law but through faith in Jesus Christ" (Galatians 2:15-16). No one will ever be justified by adhering to the Hebrew law or to any other set of rules. We are saved only by faith in God's gracious act in giving his Son, Jesus Christ.

In what ways does the church of today try to set rules? How do these rules help or hinder your life of faith?

The Components of Freedom

When Paul declared freedom from the burden of justifying one's self through obedience to the law, he set forth a broad understanding of freedom. This freedom has many components. Some of these have been realized by Christians through the ages; others have not. In some ways we are still struggling to get the people of the Christian faith to live by faith in Christ.

One component is freedom from bondage to sin. Sin will always be with us, but it is no longer our master. We do not have to do anything to atone for past sins, which are nullified by the grace of God; and we have the assurance that God will help us to overcome sin as it confronts us in the future.

A second component is freedom from religious coercion. Paul was taking a great chance by defying the other apostles, but one of the meanings of freedom in Christ is that each person is free to seek God according to the light God gives him or her. Nothing done through coercion is of any spiritual value; for God saves through grace, not through works. So to coerce persons to conform to some religious rule is to harm both the one who coerces and the one who is coerced.

In every age there are some who want to throw off the old yoke only to substitute one that reflects their own desire to prescribe prayers or dress codes or attendance schedules or rules for marital relations. These things have no effect, however, because it is grace that matters, not works. The only authority for spiritual growth is the grace of God—as revealed through the Scriptures and in the stillness of each heart.

A third component is freedom from the tyranny of a state—first of all, from a **religious** state. Since grace is paramount, it is no longer possible for any nation to determine what a person has to do to please God. Neither can any political unit force persons to be religious in a particular way, whether that unit be the Roman Empire or Iran or France or Ireland or colonial Massachusetts. Any state that tries to force persons to believe in a particular way is an enemy of grace and can only do harm to real Christian spiritual growth.

Such liberty also includes freedom from a **secular** state. Nobody can forbid worship so long as people have the courage to honor God and to face the consequences (like the Christians in Rome or in the former Soviet Union). Anyone can worship God in spirit, anytime and anywhere. The freedom to worship without forms and in any surroundings means that worship cannot be prohibited.

A fourth component is freedom from bondage to human differences. In the next chapter we will talk about how that affects the way persons relate to one another, but here the emphasis is on the effects of grace. Since faith and grace are all that count, there is no longer any religious advantage for the economically powerful. They will receive God's justification through faith, or they will be left out—just like everybody else. There is also no meaning to racial differences because race is a factor of environment and genetics, and neither of those matters. Only faith and grace matter.

Bondage is partly physical and partly of the mind, but it is mostly of the spirit. We are delivered from bondage as we walk in the spirit of the living God. Let us pray that God will deliver us from all bondage and help us express all the components of Christian freedom in our lives.

What are some other components of the freedom that comes from justification by grace?

CLOSING PRAYER
God of freedom, make us free of our bondage to self, sin, and the desire to enslave others to our views; and give us the grace to live in peace with all. We pray in the name of your Son, Jesus Christ, our Lord. Amen.

---

[1] From *Freedom Is for Freeing*, by Phillip Potter and Barbel Wartenberg Potter (General Board of Global Ministries, 1990); page 21.

Chapter Two

ADOPTED AS GOD'S CHILDREN

PURPOSE

To help us realize that adoption into God's family makes us all equally children of God

BIBLE PASSAGE

Galatians 3:1-5, 23-29

1 **You foolish Galatians! Who has bewitched you? It was before your eyes that Jesus Christ was publicly exhibited as crucified!** 2 **The only thing I want to learn from you is this: Did you receive the Spirit by doing the works of the law or by believing what you heard?** 3 **Are you so foolish? Having started with the Spirit, are you now ending with the flesh?** 4 **Did you experience so much for nothing?—if it really was for nothing.** 5 **Well then, does God supply you with the Spirit and work miracles among you by your doing the works of the law, or by your believing what you heard?** . . .

23 **Now before faith came, we were imprisoned and guarded under the law until faith would be revealed.** 24 **Therefore the law was our disciplinarian until Christ came, so that we might be justified by faith.** 25 **But now that faith has come, we are no longer subject to a disciplinarian,** 26 **for in Christ Jesus you are all children of God through**

faith. 27 As many of you as were baptized into Christ have clothed yourselves with Christ. 28 There is no longer Jew or Greek, there is no longer slave or free, there is no longer male or female; for all of you are one in Christ Jesus. 29 And if you belong to Christ, then you are Abraham's offspring, heirs according to the promise.

Galatians 4:1-7

1 My point is this: heirs, as long as they are minors, are no better than slaves, though they are the owners of all the property; 2 but they remain under guardians and trustees until the date set by the father. 3 So with us; while we were minors, we were enslaved to the elemental spirits of the world. 4 But when the fullness of time had come, God sent his Son, born of a woman, born under the law, 5 in order to redeem those who were under the law, so that we might receive adoption as children. 6 And because you are children, God has sent the Spirit of his Son into our hearts, crying, "Abba! Father!" 7 So you are no longer a slave but a child, and if a child then also an heir, through God.

CORE VERSES

God sent his Son . . . to redeem those who were under the law, so that we might receive adoption as children.

(Galatians 4:4-5)

OUR NEED

A pastor and his wife whom I know have acquired a family from a number of sources. That is, some of the children were born into the family; some were adopted; and some were foster children. To the outsider there is no discernible difference between those who were birth children and those who were adopted or fostered. They are all treated alike;

and they all act like children, their relationships with one another going through the same stages as any other group of siblings.

A story told by Chris, the mother of the lot, gave me a deeper insight into the dynamics of this family's life. She said that one day, when most of the children were still quite young, she overheard a conversation taking place on the back porch. Deanne, one of the "natural" children, was telling some visitors how she and other members of the family had been adopted. Chris was a little taken aback, so that evening at dinner she told Deanne what she had heard. Chris explained to the child that she was not adopted, that she had been carried in Chris's womb, and that her father was present when she was born.

Deanne seemed reluctant to believe Chris's account. When she finally became convinced it was true, she put her head down on the table and burst into tears. The family tried to comfort her, but Deanne was inconsolable. "Mother," she said, "you have no idea how it makes you feel to learn that you're not adopted."

Deanne is a young woman now and is no longer bothered by her status, but from her experience we all can learn that being adopted is sometimes a most desirable condition. Of course, being adopted by God is the most desirable of all. We will discuss that point in this chapter.

FAITHFUL LIVING

Paul struggled continually to find a way to describe the relationship between the people of God descended through Abraham and the new people brought in through God's grace as revealed in Jesus Christ. Paul was inspired to use the term *adoption* as a description of the process by which we all, Jew and Gentile, became one family. The first time he used the term may have been in the Bible Passage for this chapter. He was trying to help the Galatians come to an understanding of the effects of faith.

"You foolish Galatians!" (Galatians 3:1), Paul said. "Did you receive the Spirit by doing the works of the law or by believing what you heard?" (3:2). Of course it was faith (belief) that had brought the Spirit. Yet if that is true, the people of Galatia might have wondered, "Then what was the point of all that business about the commandments? If God intended for us Gentiles to be saved by grace, why did he spend all that time on the law?" Good questions!

Paul offered some answers. The law was all we had to help us understand sin, he claimed. Without the law we would not have known the extent of our transgressions. The law would not allow us to enjoy freedom from guilt, and there was really no hope life would get better. Yet we did have something to go by.

"The law was our disciplinarian" (Galatians 3:24). Under its rule we were imprisoned, guarded. Paul was saying that sometimes the law caused us to be separated from the people around us. It also kept us from going wild and committing idolatrous acts and outrages, such as human sacrifice, however. The law helped us to hold on until God sent the Son of God into the world to reveal the depth of grace to us.

Later, Paul told the faithful in Rome that God would not abandon those who kept the law. The law was not bad, it was simply insufficient. Nobody would be punished for keeping the law when the law was all there was. Indeed, those who were under the law were excellent prospects for faith. They might discover the joy of salvation if they only came to have faith (Romans 11) in Jesus Christ.

Reflecting on God's plan of salvation, Paul, a keeper of the law who had found the meaning of being kept by grace, wrote, "O the depth of the riches and wisdom and knowledge of God! How unsearchable are his judgments and how inscrutable his ways!" (Romans 11:33). Amen!

The law had its uses, but its usefulness is over. Before faith human beings were minors, slaves to the "elemental spirits of the world" (Galatians 4:3). Now we who believe in Christ are children, a part of the household of God.

What role, if any, has strict discipline played in your life?

No Longer Subject

"But now that faith has come, we are no longer subject to a disciplinarian" (Galatians 3:25). With these words Paul placed the members of the new community of faith into an innovative relationship with God and with one another. Not being subject means that we no longer have to watch or be watched every minute, and we do not have to manage our lives by someone else's pattern. We are free to explore the immense and creative possibilities of grace. We have become children of God: "So you are no longer a slave but a child, and if a child then also an heir, through Christ" (4:7).

Every person of faith is a child of God. The purpose of the whole process of grace is to put us all in the same category "so that we might receive adoption as children" (Galatians 4:5). By faith we all have been elevated from slaves to daughters and sons of God and thus sisters and brothers of one another. Nobody is barred from membership in this inclusive fellowship whose very lifeblood is love. We are subject only to God, the one who acts in love. No other bonds are placed upon us.

We have freedom as adopted children of God, yet we are called to live moral lives. How do you deal with the tension between spiritual freedom and moral responsibility?

No Longer Divided

Paul passionately and categorically identified the meaning of this new way of relating to God through faith: "There is no longer Jew or Greek, there is no longer slave or free, there is no longer male and female; for all of you are one in Christ Jesus" (Galatians 3:28). That is one of the most important comments ever made about human relationships; and it is based entirely on the coming of Jesus Christ and, through him, of justification by faith.

Human beings are no longer divided. We can never again claim to enjoy the blessings of God unless we can affirm that the same blessings are available to every person on earth. It is impossible for us to claim to love God if we do not love God's children, if we do not love those whom God loves.

We do not yet enjoy the fullness of Paul's vision, however. Even in a society that identifies itself as the most Christian on earth, there are still many people who attend church every Sunday and do not accept this fundamental Christian doctrine. And it is fundamental. The acceptance of baptism mandates the acceptance of persons of all kinds as brothers and sisters (Galatians 3:27-28). God, speaking through Paul, declared that the first result of the new life through faith is that there are no longer any differences. We are all one because we all have been adopted by the same Father and are now siblings in both faith and fact.

It will not do to say that this is only a metaphor and that God wants us to care for persons in theory, not in practice. All those references in the words of Jesus and Paul to loving our neighbors and giving crusts of bread and drinks of water—all that talk about hospitality—is based on the practical effect of our kinship in salvation. The first judgment of the success of the life of faith is not based on how much we know about doctrine or about standards of personal behavior but on how much we love other people.

Why have we resisted the clear meaning of Galatians 3:27-28 for so long?

Being adopted children in the family of God does not make us better than other people; we all are sinners saved by grace. Adoption makes us equal—not identical, just equal. The heart of the Christian matter is that there is nothing better than equality in grace.

Justification by faith is the great leveler. It places us all in the same category: sinners saved by the mercy of God's grace. Nothing we can do will get us one step closer to heaven or one step ahead of anyone else on the path of eternal life. We are either walking it together with all others who have been saved by faith or we are walking some other path, one that leads to destruction. It would indeed be a terrible thing to discover that we were not adopted into God's family.

What does it mean to you to know that you are a member of God's family?

No Longer a Slave but a Child

What differences does the change in status from slave to the world to child of God make in our relationships?

(1) Our primary relationship with God changes from dread to affection, from fear to respect. We see that God is not tyrant but parent. We do what God wants because we love God and God loves us, not because we are afraid. While God is still to be feared, we are not frightened by the divine power and majesty. Rather, we revere the One who has acted with compassion to bring us into the fold.

This role of God as Parent is not entirely new. Under the law, God was viewed as a father; but the structure of the law created a situation in which we could not please God, could not live up to our own sense of what was best and most noble. Under grace God is still the judge and still able to punish, but the measure of our righteousness or goodness is that of Jesus Christ himself. The theme is not retribution but love.

The coming of Jesus is seen as an expression of the love of God: "For God so loved the world that he gave his only Son" (John 3:16). Our love for God is an echo of the love God has given us. We are children, not subjects; and we have all the prerogatives, including nurture and support, and all the responsibilities of children.

(2) We are involved as partners in the work of God. Under the law, God seemed like a general, giving orders and commanding nations. Under grace realized through faith, God has prepared us for work by giving us gifts and tasks.

First Corinthians 3:9a illustrates this point. In speaking of the ministry of believers, Paul wrote, "For we are laborers together with God" (King James Version. Note that the New International Version and the Revised Standard Version translate 3:9a as "God's fellow workers." *The Bible in Today's English Version* uses "Partners with God." Only the NRSV translates the term as "God's servants.").

Being partners (fellow workers) with God is a consequence of our new status. We are "subject to one another" (Ephesians 5:21), but we are children of God. God has entrusted to us the building of his body, the community of faith. We are "God's field, God's building" (1 Corinthians 3:9). In the language of the quality systems of today's business world, we all are part of the process of bringing the Kingdom to reality.

(3) We participate in reconciliation, the basic tie between the divine work and the work of God's people. In Second Corinthians, Paul says, "All this is from God, who reconciled us to himself through Christ, and has given us the ministry of reconciliation" (2 Corinthians 5:18). We are to understand reconciliation as the major focus of Christian discipleship. Where people are apart from God, they are to be encouraged to open themselves to reconciliation through faith. Where they are apart from one another, they are to be encouraged to open themselves to others as God has opened himself to them. Freeing the captives, comforting the oppressed, and restoring the outcasts are integral parts of the ministry we share as children adopted into the family of God.

How do you feel about being a fellow worker with God?

CLOSING PRAYER

Dear God—parent, friend, and guide—give us the grace to become what you want your children to be and the faith to endure until the end. In the name of Christ we pray. Amen.

3

FREED TO GROW

PURPOSE

To help us explore the tension in our spiritual journeys between growing in grace and turning back

BIBLE PASSAGE

Galatians 4:8-20

8 Formerly, when you did not know God, you were enslaved to beings that by nature are not gods. 9 Now, however, that you have come to know God, or rather to be known by God, how can you turn back again to the weak and beggarly elemental spirits? How can you want to be enslaved to them again? 10 You are observing special days, and months, and seasons, and years. 11 I am afraid that my work for you may have been wasted.

12 Friends, I beg you, become as I am, for I also have become as you are. You have done me no wrong. 13 You know that it was because of a physical infirmity that I first announced the gospel to you; 14 though my condition put you to the test, you did not scorn or despise me, but welcomed me as an angel of God, as Christ Jesus. 15 What has become of the goodwill you felt? For I testify that, had it been possible, you would have torn out your eyes and given

them to me. 16 Have I now become your enemy by telling you the truth? 17 They make much of you, but for no good purpose; they want to exclude you, so that you may make much of them. 18 It is good to be made much of for a good purpose at all times, and not only when I am present with you. 19 My little children, for whom I am again in the pain of childbirth until Christ is formed in you, 20 I wish I were present with you now and could change my tone, for I am perplexed about you.

CORE VERSE

Now, however, that you have come to know God, or rather to be known by God, how can you turn back again to the weak and beggarly elemental spirits? How can you want to be enslaved to them again? (Galatians 4:9)

OUR NEED

I find these words from *Your God Is Too Small*, by J. B. Phillips, rather interesting:

All "lofty" concepts of the greatness of God need to be carefully watched lest they turn out to be mere magnifications of certain human characteristics. We may, for instance, admire the ascetic ultra-spiritual type which appears to have "a mind above" food, sexual attraction, and material comfort, for example. But if in forming a picture of the Holiness of God we are simply enlarging this spirituality and asceticism to the 'nth' degree we are forced to some peculiar conclusions. Thus we may find ourselves readily able to imagine God's interest in babies (for are they not "little bits of Heaven?"), yet unable to imagine His approval, let alone design, of the acts which led to their conception! . . .

To hold a conception of God as a mere magnified human being is to run the risk of thinking of Him as simply the Commander-in-Chief who cannot possibly spare the time to attend to the details of His subordinate's lives. Yet to have a god who is so far beyond personality and so far removed from the human context in which we alone can appreciate "values," is to have a god who is a mere bunch of perfect qualities—which means an Idea and nothing more. We need a God with the capacity to hold, so to speak, both Big and Small in His Mind at the same time. This, the Christian religion holds, is the true and satisfying conception of God revealed by Jesus Christ.[1]

Only such a God as Phillips describes can free us to be ourselves and to carry out the ministry prepared for us.

FAITHFUL LIVING

We know from reading the first chapter of the Letter to the Galatians that Paul was upset with the people in the Galatian churches. We are not certain who they were or even where they lived. Galatia was a whole territory rather than a city, and no place names are mentioned. It is as if Paul had written a letter addressed to New England. Whoever these Galatians were, he was unhappy with them.

That had not always been so. In the letter Paul reminds his readers that there was a time when they "would have torn out [their] eyes and given them to [him]" (Galatians 4:15). They had welcomed him warmly and enthusiastically. Paul was the first to proclaim the gospel to them, so they had idolized him "as an angel of God, as Christ Jesus" (4:14). The Galatians did so even though he had stayed with them because of some "physical infirmity" (4:13). They were severely tested, he said, because of his condition; but they were filled with goodwill and gladly heard the gospel.

The Galatians had turned back, however. What became of their goodwill toward him? Had they been taken in by people who "make much of" (Galatians 4:17) the Galatians but who really wanted to exclude them by putting up the barrier of circumcision and the Jewish law? Why, Paul wanted to know, were they being so foolish as to listen to those people? He just could not believe it.

In Galatians 4:18-20, Paul expresses the wish that he could be with the Galatian people. He probably thought he could influence them in person, could overcome the problems that arose in his absence.

We can almost see the emotions washing over Paul as he wrote the letter. He was quite irritated with the Galatians, but he did not want them to think that was his only feeling. Paul wanted to defend the gospel, but he also wanted to defend himself. He would like to love them back into the fold, but he felt like scolding them too.

How human Paul seems, how troubled by the loss of friendship. Yet how carefully he continued to represent the gospel and to cultivate the presence of God in himself and in his readers. No wonder God chose him as the one to communicate the faith to the wider world.

Have you ever been disappointed at how a friendship turned out? If so, what were the circumstances?

The People Turn Back

The gospel Paul preached may have been unique at this point in the development of Christianity. He and others who were a part of his missionary efforts might have been the only ones preaching justification by faith without the law. Even the apostles and other leaders in Judea were suspicious of Paul's ministry—as late as the Jerusalem Conference mentioned in Acts 15. God used Paul, the regenerated firebrand, to put the new church on the right track.

There had been some concessions to the "Gentile" gospel Paul preached. The letter that was sent to the church at

Antioch (Acts 15:22-29) indicated that those in power still wanted to impose rules on the Gentile converts, however. Thus, it may have been people saying they were representatives of the apostles who were trying to persuade the Galatians to return to traditional Jewish practices.

After warning the Galatians against allowing Jewish Christians to entangle them in ritual practices, Paul went on to warn them against turning "back again to the weak and beggarly elemental spirits" (Galatians 4:9a). What were elemental spirits?

In classical Greek thought the elements were air, fire, earth, and water. Later the term was enlarged to include also the "spirits" that were behind the elements: gods of the trees and streams, astrological deities, angels, and so forth. The Gentile Christians may have originally been adherents of religions that worshiped these spirits. Such religions often included prediction of the future with astrology and/or the entrails of animals. In Christ, however, these spirits and religions are seen as mere superstitions.

Paul again referred to the Jewish faith, to the harvest and new moon festivals and sabbath observances (both seven days and seven years), as well as to days of atonement and other seasonal celebrations. Some prophets had also objected to feasts: "I hate, I despise your festivals, and . . . solemn assemblies" (Amos 5:21). Jesus criticized some restrictions related to the sabbath (Mark 2:23-28; John 5:1-18). Paul was disturbed that special days might take the place of real worship. He warned the people not to turn back but to continue in the way they began, the way of the Spirit.

What practices, if any, do you know of that seem like those to which Paul objected?

Turning Back in Our Time

By a careful reading of the letters of Paul, we can see many areas in which turning back from faith and grace can endanger our spiritual health. As we read, we will discover that many of our most cherished practices are part of the problem. The tension between turning back and spiritual growth is often caused by the anxiety we have in giving up our icons of church life.

(1) We can turn back in worship. In a conversation with a woman of Samaria, Jesus said, "The hour is coming, and is now here, when the true worshipers will worship the Father in spirit and truth, for the Father seeks such as these to worship him. God is spirit, and those who worship him must worship in spirit and truth" (John 4:23-24).

We want our worship to be beautiful and majestic and inspiring or exciting and dramatic and moving—perhaps both. Yet how easy it is to substitute the liturgies of the past or the entertainments of today for true spiritual worship. Each congregation must find its own style, but every worship service must have a place for the Spirit of God to speak to the spirits of men, women, and children.

(2) We can turn back from the spiritual truth that we all are equal in grace. That has happened so many times. One wonders how the United States could ever have justified enslaving Africans or killing thousands of native people in the name of Christianity. In a more modern setting, our culture blandly consigns persons to inferior places in society because they do not speak English or are old or have a physically challenging condition. For Christians to do so is to turn back, to forsake the faith.

Churches and persons must be inclusive. Racially separated congregations may be "comfortable," but they do not express the fullness of grace. Discrimination against women in choosing clergy and other church leaders may suit the expectations of some people, but it does not suit the gospel. These and other exclusions do not allow the fulfillment of the spiritual potential of *any* of the members of the body. We do not reach our true capacity for ministry until we are one in the Spirit.

(3) **We can turn back by the repression of new ideas.** We can easily forget that the heart of the body of Christ is the variety of gifts its members offer. In so doing, we may reject people who bring new methods or new ways of thinking. One reason our churches do not grow is that we have such a stagnant definition of Christian discipleship; we cannot accept those who go about the faith in a way different from that to which we are accustomed.

Some church growth experts have said that the way to grow is to attract persons who are like one another. That may make a specific congregation grow, but it surely inhibits the growth of the whole body of Christ. "Many gifts" means the opportunity for many avenues of the Spirit. Suppressing gifts means hindering the Spirit.

(4) **We can turn back by spending our time judging rather than encouraging.** As we have seen, Paul warned over and over that judging the behavior of others is a detriment to the full realization of the spiritual potential of the fellowship. He said that many acts are subject to interpretation, depending on our background. He called on us to help one another instead of condemning one another.

I have heard people say that they could not go to another church because the music there was so "loud." I have heard persons criticized for not wearing a tie to church. I have found myself wondering aloud why some people do not know how to act in certain social situations. All of us are going against the Spirit when we say such things. For life in the Spirit is more concerned about the things of the Spirit—love, peace, joy, kindness—than about the things of the flesh— dress, grammar, musical taste, or personal appearance.

(5) **We can lose ground by turning back from righteous living.** While this may include everything we have already said, it also implies more than that. There is a need for per-

sonal purity, freedom from the defilement of the self, that cannot be overlooked. In our day it is particularly hard to maintain purity; there are so many opportunities for activities that damage our morals, our bodies, or our minds. Therefore, life today requires more discipline of the physical self in order to free the spiritual self.

The list could go on. These items only illustrate the ways in which we can turn back from the call of the Spirit and give up possibilities for growth in grace, growth that will satisfy our spiritual needs and build up the body of Christ.

What other ways of turning back from full spirituality can you name?

Times of Turning Back

There are times when turning back is especially tempting. For the people of Galatia, the period when Paul left and other authority figures arrived was such a time. For us it might be one of the following times:

At the Change Points of Life:
when we enter high school;
when we get married or have our first child;
when we move to a new town or gain new friends;
when the children have gone;
when retirement comes.

All the changes of life may involve changes in our spiritual habits.

When Commitment Wanes:
when we are disappointed in our church leaders;
when we begin to feel spiritually drained;
when we experience personal loss (loved ones or cherished objects or objectives).

When Competing Loyalties Arise:
  the claims of a family or the rigors of a career;
  social needs and the people we choose to fill them;
  addictive drugs or lifestyles.

All the above are moments when the drive toward spiritual growth may be in jeopardy. Paul would be astonished at the variety of ways we can turn back in the twenty-first century, but he would not be surprised at the fact that we do so. Maintaining the integrity of life in the Spirit is difficult in any age. The only hope we have is that the grace of God goes before us and the love of God protects us. We will need all the prayer support and help from one another we can get, in addition to the grace and mercy of God, if we are to be the people of God for this time and place.

CLOSING PRAYER
God of spirit, God of life, keep us in your path and strengthen us for your service. In Jesus' name we pray. Amen.

---

[1] From *Your God Is Too Small*, by J.B. Phillips (The Macmillan Company, 1964); pages 44–45.

Chapter Four

ENABLED TO BEAR FRUIT

PURPOSE

To help us express the joy of Christian freedom in the fruits of the Spirit

BIBLE PASSAGE

Galatians 5:1, 13-26

1 **For freedom Christ has set us free. Stand firm, therefore, and do not submit again to a yoke of slavery.** . . .

13 **For you were called to freedom, brothers and sisters; only do not use your freedom as an opportunity for self-indulgence, but through love become slaves to one another.** 14 **For the whole law is summed up in a single commandment, "You shall love your neighbor as yourself." 15 If, however, you bite and devour one another, take care that you are not consumed by one another.**

16 **Live by the Spirit, I say, and do not gratify the desires of the flesh. 17 For what the flesh desires is opposed to the Spirit, and what the Spirit desires is opposed to the flesh; for these are opposed to each other, to prevent you from doing what you want. 18 But if you are led by the Spirit, you are not subject to the law. 19 Now the works of the flesh are obvious: fornication, impurity, licentiousness, 20 idolatry,**

sorcery, enmities, strife, jealousy, anger, quarrels, dissensions, factions, 21 envy, drunkenness, carousing, and things like these. I am warning you, as I warned you before: those who do such things will not inherit the kingdom of God.

22 By contrast, the fruit of the Spirit is love, joy, peace, patience, kindness, generosity, faithfulness, 23 gentleness, and self-control. There is no law against such things. 24 And those who belong to Christ Jesus have crucified the flesh with its passions and desires. 25 If we live by the Spirit, let us also be guided by the Spirit. 26 Let us not become conceited, competing against one another, envying one another.

CORE VERSES

The fruit of the Spirit is love, joy, peace, patience, kindness, generosity, faithfulness, gentleness, and self-control.

(Galatians 5:22-23)

OUR NEED

John Wesley, the founder of Methodism, saw clearly the relationship between what we do and who we are. Even for one who greatly valued "doing," he saw that "being" is the primary condition; the fruits of the Spirit are expressions of who we are in Christ. Here are some thoughts from one of his sermons:

> Even in the infancy of the church God divided [the gifts] with a sparing hand. 'Were all' even then 'prophets?' Were all 'workers of miracles? Had all the gifts of healing? Did all speak with tongues?' No, in no wise. Perhaps not one in a thousand. . . . It was therefore for a more excellent purpose than this that 'they were all filled with the Holy Ghost.'

It was to give them (what none can deny to be essential to all Christians in all ages) 'the mind which was in Christ', those holy 'fruits of the Spirit' which 'whosoever hath not is none of his'; to fill them with 'love, joy, peace, long-suffering, gentleness, goodness'; to endue them with 'faith' (perhaps it might be rendered 'fidelity'), with 'meekness and temperance'; to enable them to 'crucify the flesh, with its affections and lusts' (Gal. 5:22), its passions and desires; and, in consequences of that *inward change,* to fulfill all *outward* righteousness, to 'walk as Christ also walked', in the 'work of faith, the patience of hope, the labour of love' (1 Thess. 1:3).[1]

In this chapter, we will look at what enables a person truly to live out the faith.

FAITHFUL LIVING

In the opening verse of our Bible Passage, Paul warns that we may miss the joy of the new life in Christ if we let the freedom it brings be wasted in mere self-indulgence (Galatians 5:13). Paul then told what freedom in Christ is: the freedom to love.

Christian freedom is realized when believers "become slaves to one another" (Galatians 5:13). What a delightful paradox. To emphasize the point, Paul added, "For the whole law is summed up in a single commandment, 'You shall love your neighbor as yourself.' " (5:14). Jesus quoted from Leviticus 19:18 in much the same way (Matthew 22:39). Both the Lord and his apostle meant that the law is superseded or replaced by love. The essence of Christian faith comes to expression in love, not as a ritual adherence to law but as a way of life.

In becoming slaves to one another, for example, the mutual love of the members of the body is lived out. Such slavery means being concerned about feelings and needs; it means caring for relationships rather than for rules; and it means knowing that the love of God is best expressed through the love of people. Life in the Spirit is life that fulfills the law—because it comes from the presence of God within. The presence of the Spirit enables Christians to bear fruit. This religion is not conformity to but expression of the new life, the new love in Christ. Thus Paul said, "If you are led by the Spirit, you are not subject to the law" (Galatians 5:18). To paraphrase a famous football coach, Love is not the best thing, it is the only thing.

The freedom comes from the ability to go with our feelings instead of constantly having to check legal regulations. If our feelings come from the experience of grace, mediated through the Spirit of God, and are based on love, we can rely on them to direct our behavior: "If we live by the Spirit, let us also be guided by the Spirit" (Galatians 5:25).

The joy of the new life is that external actions and internal feelings have been joined. God has bridged the gap, and we have become one in our "personhood" as well as in Christ. What we are and what we do are the same if we genuinely live in the Spirit. Being and doing are united. As Paul expressed it in Philippians, "For it is God who is at work in you, enabling you both to will and to work for his good pleasure" (Philippians 2:13).

What are some benefits of this new freedom? Some dangers?

Self-indulgences

Having stressed the opportunities of grace, Paul spelled out what he meant by self-indulgence. We can divide the forms of self-indulgence into four broad categories. Each kind of indulgence is a danger to the newly created spiritual self and may prevent us from bearing the fruit of the Spirit.

(1) The first category is sexual excess. The numerous references to matters of sex probably do not mean that sexual indulgence is more damaging than other indulgences, only that it is more prevalent. Reading the New Testament leads us to conclude that the first-century church was much like today's: More people erred in sexual matters than in any other; and sex is a comprehensive issue. Like Jesus, Paul identified not only fornication but also impure thought as misuse of sexuality. He also mentioned the enjoyment of sexual titillation (licentiousness).

From this and other passages it is clear that sexual problems are not just legal, having to do with marriage laws and property rights, but also spiritual. Sex can become so absorbing that it displaces other objectives. We have ample evidence of that in our own time: So-called adult books, movies, and DVDs sell by the millions. Sex, like other gifts of God, is good in itself; but the single-minded pursuit of sex impedes the realization of life in the Spirit.

(2) The second category is idolatry. Idolatry is worship of or devotion to something that is not worthy of such respect. Sorcery is connected with idolatry; it is the belief that material things have power that can be manipulated for our benefit. Idolatry may be the most prevalent yet unacknowledged hindrance to true faith in our time.

Contemporary idolatry does not center on graven images, but it occurs all the same. Think about it: We call public figures "idols" when people become obsessed with them. Sports, music and entertainment, politics, and even religion have produced their share of idols. At times this form of idolatry causes hysteria and bizarre behavior. But then, so does the obsession with money (another idol) or houses or recreational vehicles or status or family. Our church buildings can become idols when their appearance and furnishings become more important than the worship they are built to house. We are casual and often unconscious idolaters, failing to understand that any form of self-indulgence can become an obsession.

Nor is all the sorcery practiced by those who call themselves Satanists. We allow ourselves to enter into sorcery when we invoke the name of some celebrity in order to sell soap, clothing, cars, pain relievers, or religious objects (books, handkerchiefs, therapy). Our idols become means to control people. How far from the Kingdom we stray!

What symptoms of idolatry have you found in yourself?

(3) The third category is contentiousness. Contentiousness ranges all the way from children seeking attention by misbehaving to adults picking fights with other church members just to prove how smart or powerful they are. Quarrels, dissensions, jealousy, and envy are products of self-centeredness.

When we focus on self instead of on God, we are liable to attack anyone who stands in our way or disagrees with us. When we are like that, we force others to seek our permission; and we are not very permissive.

I remember a sudden eruption of anger by a longtime church member in a board meeting one evening. A few days later he came by the office and said, "I'm sorry. It's just that I get so mad when Robert talks in that superior way. I let it get to me." This man was a victim of envy. Robert was the symbol of all the privileged persons in the world to him, and he wanted to attack Robert every time he and Robert were in the same room. In time, he and Robert became friends; he faced the truth about himself and was able to apologize for his contentious behavior.

Contentious people are part of every group, of every church. We often kowtow to them because we do not want a confrontation, so they never have to face the effects of their own behavior. Paul included those persons in the same category as fornicators and idolaters. While they may get their way, they never know the joy of life in the Spirit.

Factionalism is the bane of the body of Christ. We know that each person has a unique relationship with God and that all are gifted differently. Yet we still want to categorize everyone by criteria of our own devising (which we usually think are based on the Scriptures) and to expel those who do not meet our standards. It is this judgment that creates factions—and we always consider our faction to be the best one.

Quarrels and dissensions may lead to factionalism. When we cannot agree on the color of the cloth for the altar or on the proper way to serve the Lord's Supper or on the kind of music to play at the worship service, we are only expressing the varieties of human preference. When we let those things keep us from loving one another, we have become self-indulgent, however.

If sexual immorality was the most prevalent sin of the early church, factionalism must have been second. Every letter Paul wrote begged for unity, pleaded for love. He tried to tell the local churches that different ways of serving, ways of worship, ways of dealing with the laws, and ways of being spiritual were the result of legitimate differences between people; but none of the differences should interfere with the expression of love. Love is the crowning glory of the church; and no style of worship, theological system, or regimen of activities can replace it. Disagree with one another—by all means. Separate from one another—never! Nothing is as important as being the community of faith, the one body of Christ.

(4) The fourth category is carousing. Finally, Paul warned the church about "carousing," which means getting so caught up in celebrations that we lose the focus of life. We all know that carousing means going to places that cater to boisterous behavior and/or places that feature alcohol and other drugs. Yet people can also carouse at a football game or at a barbecue in the back yard. Some can even carouse at church. They can be drunk on the Spirit. They become so worked up that they cannot see the mission of the body because they are indulging themselves in personal spiritual expression. Not for nothing did Paul say that "since you are eager for spiritual gifts, strive to excel in them for building up the church" (1 Corinthians 14:12).

Everything we do should build up the church. Paul repeated that admonition over and over. What he meant was that any form of self-indulgence threatens the very foundation of our spiritual life together. Not only that, but "as I warned you before: those who do such things will not inherit the kingdom of God" (Galatians 5:21). By acting self-indulgently, we risk not only the loss of the fruit of the Spirit but also the loss of heaven.

Why did Paul place so much stress on the church?

The Fruit of the Spirit

The fruit of the Spirit flows out of the new union with Christ. It is the consequence of a "new life." In our Bible Passage and in other letters, Paul described some of the characteristics of this fruitful life. In comparison with this list, the one in Colossians 3:12 includes "kindness" and "patience" and adds "compassion," "humility," and "meekness." In Romans 14:17, we also find "peace and joy"; and "righteousness" is added.

These marks of the new life are meant to contrast with the "works of the flesh." The contrast is both inward and outward. The new life involves changes in one's internal relationship with God and self and in one's internal and external relationships with others.

The New Testament reflects an attitude toward others that is far advanced beyond its period and place of origin.

Sadly, it has yet to be implemented. When Paul recorded that God has planned that reconciled persons will be peaceful, kind, patient with one another (tolerant?), gentle, and compassionate, he went against every standard of the world of competition and power. The Christian standard is love; and the Christian assessment of any action or attitude is straightforward: Does it conform to the standard of love?

The fruits of the Spirit Paul set forth allow us to be with others in joy. Together we can express who and whose we are, people renewed by the grace of God. If what we do is done in and for love—is done in the Spirit—it will be right before God and edifying for all.

It is tragic when people believe that the new freedom in Christ involves a lack of restraint on our personal actions. Rather, it involves a new way of looking at others. We express the essence of Christian freedom when we live in love, and the love of God enables us to bear the fruits of the Spirit.

CLOSING PRAYER

God of all, awaken us to the potential for joy in the loving fellowship that your Spirit makes possible. Help us bear fruit together. In the name of Jesus Christ, our Lord, we pray. Amen.

---

[1] From "Spiritual Christianity," by John Wesley, in *John Wesley's Sermons: An Anthology,* edited by Albert C. Outler and Richard P. Heitzenrater (Abingdon Press, 1991); pages 98–99.

Chapter Five

CHALLENGED TO LOVE

PURPOSE

To encourage us to nurture and support people, both within and without the community of faith, through the Spirit of Christ

BIBLE PASSAGE

Galatians 6:1-10, 14-18

1 My friends, if anyone is detected in a transgression, you who have received the Spirit should restore such a one in a spirit of gentleness. Take care that you yourselves are not tempted. 2 Bear one another's burdens, and in this way you will fulfill the law of Christ. 3 For if those who are nothing think they are something, they deceive themselves. 4 All must test their own work; then that work, rather than their neighbor's work, will become a cause for pride. 5 For all must carry their own loads.

6 Those who are taught the word must share in all good things with their teacher.

7 Do not be deceived; God is not mocked, for you reap whatever you sow. 8 If you sow to your own flesh, you will reap corruption from the flesh; but if you sow to the Spirit, you will reap eternal life from the Spirit. 9 So let us not grow

weary in doing what is right, for we will reap at harvest time, if we do not give up. 10 So then, whenever we have an opportunity, let us work for the good of all, and especially for those of the family of faith. . . . 14 May I never boast of anything except the cross of our Lord Jesus Christ, by which the world has been crucified to me, and I to the world. 15 For neither circumcision nor uncircumcision is anything; but a new creation is everything! 16 As for those who will follow this rule—peace be upon them, and mercy, and upon the Israel of God.

17 From now on, let no one make trouble for me; for I carry the marks of Jesus branded on my body.

18 May the grace of our Lord Jesus Christ be with your spirit, brothers and sisters. Amen.

CORE VERSE

Let us work for the good of all, and especially for those of the family of faith. (Galatians 6:10)

OUR NEED

Over the years of writing Bible studies, I have often encountered Scripture that speaks about love. Since love is the dominant theme of the New Testament, that is not surprising. What is surprising is the number of people who write to protest against too much emphasis on love.

The letters follow a similar pattern. They point out that loving God is more crucial than loving people (which is not exactly what the Bible says), and they ask that more be said about the responsibility of persons to do things that will make them more lovable. The central theme is, "Why do you always talk about love and concern for people when so many of them are full of evil and sin?"

My only defense for such a position is that it seems to be the very foundation of the new life in Christ. God loved us in just this way, without regard for our suitability for such affection, when he sent Jesus into the world to reconcile us to himself and to one another. The only possible conclusion we can draw from Scripture is that we are expected to show the same regard for others, whether we think them worthy or not.

Our human perspective on love, that it has to be earned, is just not sufficient for the new life in Jesus Christ. In order to understand the nature of Christian love, we must look to the example that God gave us, not to the world. We will talk about this love in this chapter.

FAITHFUL LIVING

The ancient Greek language had many words for love, each carrying a slightly different meaning. The word *eros* (from which we get our term *erotic*) was commonly used for sexual love. It is not found in the New Testament. A second word, *phileo*, referred to love between friends; the word is used occasionally in the New Testament. *Philia* meant social love and is used only once in Scripture. *Philadelphia* meant love between brothers or sisters (as in Philadelphia, the city of brotherly love) and is sometimes used to refer to love between Christians.

Of the many other words for love, only one, *agape* [ah-GAH-pay], is widely used in the New Testament. It is the word of choice when referring to God's love for human beings, the love of humans for God, or the love of those in Christ for one another or for those outside the faith.

Not only is *agape* the most commonly used word for love in the New Testament, it is a word hardly used in classical Greek outside the New Testament. One can almost say that it is the special word for love in its Christian meaning. We should therefore understand the kind of love it implies.

Agape connotes a love that is spontaneously and freely given. It does not need a response and is not dependent on the worth of the recipient. *Agape* does not impose conditions. It is offered for the benefit of the object of love, and the giver does not expect a reward or acknowledgment. It is not self-indulgent. Since it is so much more than ordinary human love, some have called *agape* "divine love."

In fact, *agape* is precisely the type of love described with such care in 1 Corinthians 13: It is patient and kind. It is not envious or resentful. It does not seek to manipulate persons to get its own way. "It bears all things, believes all things, hopes all things, endures all things" (1 Corinthians 13:7). *Agape* is extraordinary love.

What kinds of love have affected you? In what ways?

The Origin of Love

God helped the writers of the New Testament to express the remarkable love revealed in Jesus Christ by the use of a word that was not burdened with other meanings. It always meant the highest form of love, undiluted by the other ideas that gathered around the more general terms of the time (or the ones we use today). Why a new word, *agape*?

From the beginning, the Christians understood that the new revelation God had made through Christ was that God is fundamentally love. They saw this love in Jesus; and since Jesus is God, they saw that God is love. The Gospel writer John made a special point of explaining love; and the letters of John declare its supreme value. In every case the same Greek word, *agape,* is used to convey God's love.

The writings of Paul serve to make the meaning of love clear. It is the very nature of God to love; that is the source of grace. God's love makes justification possible. In this experience human beings find the meaning of love and are able to love because God has revealed what love is by loving us. This new understanding of love could never have been reached through human reason. It could only have come from God.

Through learning about love as revealed in Christ, people are able to love God. It is love of God and not knowledge about love that matters: "Anyone who claims to know something does not yet have the necessary knowledge; but anyone who loves God is known by him" (1 Corinthians 8:2-3).

This same love, *agape,* as a product of reconciliation, is the fruit of the Spirit. It is not only the basic route to God, it is the normal response of justified persons to one another and to those not yet aware of God's grace: "Owe no one anything, except to love one another" (Romans 13:8). "For in Christ Jesus neither circumcision nor uncircumcision counts for anything; the only thing that counts is faith working through love" (Galatians 5:6).

What differences do you see between **agape** *love and that practiced by most people today?*

Helping One Another

The competitiveness that is normal to human beings often leads us to feel superior when someone else fails. Paul warned Christians not to act that way when others were in the wrong: "If anyone is detected in a transgression, you who have received the Spirit should restore such a one in a spirit of gentleness" (Galatians 6:1). Paul challenged us to behave like persons reconciled to God rather than like those pursuing customary ways of judgment and censure.

Paul's words demonstrate that love is not just an ideal, it is a practical demonstration of the fruit of grace and faith. In spite of the strong moral and theological position Paul took, he affirmed that the expression of loving concern is more appropriate than rebuke. That insight (He did not always observe it himself.) could have only come from the Spirit of God. Such love is unknown except among those who have been reconciled to God.

There follows a warning that is as pertinent today as when it was written: "Take care that you yourselves are not tempted" (Galatians 6:1). The expression of compassion for the erring must not lead to personal involvement in the error. We should recognize that we too are subject to temptation and are to extend forgiveness even as we maintain our self-control.

"Bear one another's burdens, and in this way you will fulfill the law of Christ" (Galatians 6:2), Paul added. He surely did not mean just the burdens laid upon the Christian community by those who opposed it but also the burdens that each one bore because of poor decisions and imperfect acts. If Christians cannot help the fallen, then where is there help for them? Exactly that quality has both gratified and mystified the people of God. We want to help and to correct at the same time. How difficult it is to remember that in the love of Christ help comes first. Loving and not judging best expresses the divine love we have gained through Christ.

How would you evaluate your expressions of Christian love toward those who have fallen?

Carrying Our Own Load

Just in case the Christian feels that expressing love to others will free him or her of the obligation to maintain moral and spiritual standards, Paul said, "All must test their own work; then that work, rather than their neighbor's work, will become a cause for pride. For all must carry their own loads" (Galatians 6:4-5).

The point here is that we cannot take any comfort in the fact that a lot of other people are failing to live up to the standard of love. God does not "grade on the curve." We are expected to keep the standard of God's love in front of us and to try to sustain it even if no one else even gets close. We must be concerned with our own faithfulness.

We cannot hold anyone else to the same standard we have, however. Each must answer to his or her own conscience. It is entirely possible that some will be expected to live more carefully than others in some ways because they understand better what the standards are. Nobody has to meet the standards God sets for us except us. Even if we do meet them, we have no right to judge others for failing to meet our standards.

"Do not be deceived; God is not mocked, for you reap whatever you sow" (Galatians 6:7). That observation applies to us all, but God makes the application. We do not have the responsibility for judging the achievement of others. That right belongs to God alone.

One of the shocks of love is to realize that we must bear with the failures of others while still carrying the responsibility for our own actions. We do not gain merit, do not earn God's favor, for acting like Christians. God loves us, and life in the Spirit is its own reward.

How do you feel when you see persons failing to keep what you believe to be God's standards? What should you do?

Keep up the Good Work

Paul knew that being a Christian is not all joy and peace. The very nature of the faith is so opposite to the common pattern of human behavior that it is bound to be something of a strain to sustain. Remember how Paul said that he could not do what he should and was always doing something he knew he should not? There is a danger in that for all of us.

Like Martin Luther, we can imagine that "the devil has all the best tunes" and despair of "keeping on keeping on." Like the people of Galatia, we can realize that some of our fellow Christians are critical of our tolerance and tell us that our beliefs are wrong. It is a temptation to throw up our hands and say, "I just don't care anymore."

In response, Paul recommended that we "not grow weary in doing what is right" (Galatians 6:9). By that he clearly meant that the good we do and the people we support are all part of the love we have received from God through faith and now offer back to God and others insofar as we can. However irritated we may become with our meager results or with ungrateful recipients, we have only one option: Keep on doing good.

To be sure that we would not miss the point (Notice how often Paul said the same thing two or three times if he thought we might be reluctant to believe it?), he went on to say, "Whenever we have an opportunity, let us work for the good of all, and especially for those of the family of faith" (Galatians 6:10). Two things are worth noting about this statement: First, Paul did not say work for the "right" of all but "for the good of all." It is the good for which we are responsible. God will take care of the rightness.

Second, some have claimed that Paul meant we are to do good only for members of the family of faith and that he did not mention service to those outside. It is clear in this passage that he spoke of both, for he first called for doing good for all and then added a special word about doing good for fellow Christians. Or from a different perspective, perhaps, Paul knew that some of us like to help the public poor but have little regard for those we see every Sunday.

To what good are you drawn? How is your interest realized?

Challenged to Love

A good way to end this study is with the challenge to love one another. We have been studying Paul's letter to the Galatians, and nothing is more typical of the apostle than the emphasis on love.

Such an emphasis may be a bit contrary to our picture of the feisty missionary to the Gentiles. But something amazing had happened to Paul: He had encountered the Lord on the Damascus Road. Paul was completely transformed by the presence of God in his life. If he had come to the Christian faith in a more casual way, as many of us did, he might never have been open to the outpouring of the Spirit of God that made him such a great spokesperson for the faith. Paul had been a champion of the law, but he became a witness to grace. He had viciously attacked those he saw as enemies of God, but he pleaded for love toward those who were weak. Paul had a profound vision of the grace and love expressed in God's plan of salvation.

We can be grateful for that vision. It is the glory of this life and of the life to come. When we participate in the grace of justification and reconciliation and walk the path of love, we—like Paul—are free to be God's true representatives, members of the body of Christ.

CLOSING PRAYER

Dear God, open our eyes and our affections so that we may serve you and your people through the love you have given us. In Jesus' name we pray. Amen.
